THE PORTAGE POETRY SERIES

Series Titles

Messengers of the Gods
Kathryn Gahl

After the 8-Ball
Colleen Alles

Careful Cartography
Devon Bohm

Broken On the Wheel
Barbara Costas-Biggs

Sparks and Disperses
Cathleen Cohen

Holding My Selves Together
Margaret Rozga

Lost and Found Departments
Heather Dubrow

Marginal Notes
Alfonso Brezmes

The Almost-Children
Cassondra Windwalker

Meditations of a Beast
Kristine Ong Muslim

Praise for
Kathryn Gahl

Messengers of the Gods is a masterpiece of poetic craft and deeply felt truths, thanks to Kathryn Gahl's ability to dance with words in an alchemy of form and style. Her impressive poetic reach shows mastery of the craft, whereby the physical form works in conjunction with sound to deepen and widen meaning. These poems are "a murmur in a trombone throat / a mournful joy," and will "play as long as you do" (Big Band). Gahl might well be speaking of the poetic process in "a union of parts / to shape the craving" (When the Kissing). This is poetry for poets as it taps an inner bard, yet it is poetry for people, too, highlighting fondue, farmhouse kitchens, and sunflowers. Feel her words "rise from the page / like high notes of a flute" (Sister) and bask in Gahl's surprising perspective, such as "floored boards hugging one another, floating, giving in to the pressure of dancers" (Floored). Readers will give in, too, to Gahl and her unique voice.

—Sylvia Cavanaugh, author of *Icarus, Anthropology of Addiction*

In Kathryn Gahl's stunning new collection, *Messengers of the Gods*, a river of music and dance flows through her poems. She carries us in waves of enchanting language, graceful imagery, and an intoxicating energy of rhythm. With vivid descriptions throughout, her extraordinary poems sing, like "a trumpet spun of gold, wet kisses." These are life-giving stories about the authentic, real moments of love, loss, connection, and family, as well as the beauty of art and nature. These are moments not always written down, "what can rip a heart," and yet, Gahl shares them with us. She invites us into the house of memory, "where we inhale pain and exhale love," and we hang onto her every word. Perhaps we are all just experiencing a "brief glory traveling through space and time," on this earth. "Come dance with me / connect with me," Gahl implores, and we do.

—Cristina M. R. Norcross, Editor of *Blue Heron Review*
author of *The Sound of a Collective Pulse*

If born into a world void of sound, reading Kathryn Gahl's poetry would offer all one needs to tap their feet, for her lines give rhythm to silence with each intimate memory of summer tans, paper towels, ambulances, pandemics, log splitting, loon diving, parenting, love, and loss. *Messengers of the Gods* is the song we all need to hear right now in this unsettling world to "teach our cells new moves," as Gahl writes, to become Iris and fly, to hold loves beyond the grave, and, most important, to dream.

—Jodie Mortag, Lakeland University

Kathryn Gahl's *Messengers of the Gods* journeys through the dance of life. Tightly crafted images move across the page with rhythm and metaphor and "A journey of a thousand miles begins with a single step./ and so, you enter the dance studio and watch/ The speech of feet and think/ let this be boundless...." Gahl goes deep, sharing poems of mystery, heartache, love, and loss, returning to dance for comfort because "The real opponent is time, however, so/ yoga up/ release the grief/ advance the divine/ and down the carrots." This is an exquisite read, with a masterful use of language, celebrating movement with words.

—Annette Langlois Grunseth
author of *Combat and Campus: Writing Through War*

Kathryn Gahl's *Messengers of the Gods* rings with music, accompanied by dance. Her poems proclaim "all love is dance," proclaim "my body is my joy." They take us to the childhood barn, the family kitchen, a daughter's cell, many dance floors, a trip to Menards, the interiors of memory, and the throes of desire. The poems are tender and wise, rich with the human-ness of our lives, wry and honest, naming "a bluebird fighting a crow for the last speck."

—C. Kubasta, author of *Abjectification* and *Of Covenants*

Kathryn Gahl's poems are filled with the sweet but hard liquor of life. With delicious details, she writes of dancing amidst domesticity, of rural living, of taverns and school busses. There are grease guns and chainsaws, and "... a cuddle-mad moon", all showing her skill as a wordsmith. For me, there is a deep resonance, especially with poems of her mother, the endless and often thankless work. Gahl is a poet of great skill and heart.

—Karla Huston: Wisconsin Poet Laureate 2017–2018
author of *Grief Bone* and *A Theory of Lipstick*

In *Messengers of the Gods*, Kathryn Gahl holds out her hand and invites us to dance. "A journey of a thousand miles begins with a single step." The poet's words will carry you across steamy dance floors, childhood kitchens, farms, hospitals, and even prisons. Like the dance itself, these poems will work you. Let them.

—Lisa Vihos, Poet Laureate of Sheboygan, Wisconsin
author of *The Lone Snake: The Story of Sofonisba Anguissola*

Messengers of the Gods

New & Selected Poems

Kathryn Gahl

Cornerstone Press
Stevens Point, Wisconsin

Cornerstone Press, Stevens Point, Wisconsin 54481
Copyright © 2022 Kathryn Gahl
www.uwsp.edu/cornerstone

Printed in the United States of America by
Point Print and Design Studio, Stevens Point, Wisconsin 54481

Library of Congress Control Number: 2021953235
ISBN: 978-1-7377390-6-7

Cornerstone Press titles are produced in courses and internships offered by the
Department of English at the University of Wisconsin–Stevens Point.

DIRECTOR & PUBLISHER   EXECUTIVE EDITOR   SENIOR EDITORS
Dr. Ross K. Tangedal   Jeff Snowbarger   Lexie Neeley & Monica Swinick

SENIOR PRESS ASSISTANTS
Kala Buttke, Emma Fisher, Gavrielle McClung

PRESS STAFF
Rosie Acker, Rhiley Block, Grace Dahl, Patrick Fogarty, Kyra Goedken, Brett Hill,
Seth Kundinger, Amanda Leibham, Pachia Moua, Cassie Ress, Annika Rice, Abbi Rohde,
Bethany Webb

in memory of my parents

Also by Kathryn Gahl

Life Drawing Class
The Velocity of Love
Hard Life, Hard Love
The Yellow Toothbrush: A Memoir

Poems

— Mood —

— Frame —

— Timing —

— Becoming —

— Being —

— Dreaming —

True ease in writing comes from art, not chance,
As those move easiest who have learn'd to dance.

—Alexander Pope, *An Essay on Criticism*

— Mood —

At the Tea Dance

In the pale
slant
of afternoon light

coming in
the
south window

her eyes set
on him
with gratitude

for he was
a man
who could dance

Big Band

I am a saxophone smokin'
a murmur in a trombone throat
I am mournful joy
a skipped beat, held slide
a trumpet spun of gold, wet kisses
swish and swash of sunlight

In my player's cheeks I am agony
masquerading as frenzy
a finger roll, hold me baby,
trot my fox and waltz my wish

Make me nothing but pure air
a brassy queen, pretty lady
whose feet scramble in East Coast
the sugar tuck in West Coast
lungs bold with noise.

Sequence me with mad drums
a bass plucking itself clean
the clarinet's chatter, bumblebee glee
          tongues speaking
                    in clatter and drool
                              drawing out sm-o-o-o-ch

I will be your undertone with no place
for oboes or mink coats, only summer nights and
winter storm, a solo floating the floorboards
blues and breeze me
tease me, dance me
in lemony dawn and deep afternoon,
lead me to a Sunday
kind of love, leaves and grass, clouds, infinite sky

I am wind, hum, cymbals burning,
water falling luminous and loud
a roaring rise to electrify
spine, ankle, knee, and neck

I will play as long as you do

The First Time

the first time
your mother held you.
the first time
you heard your father laugh.

all that

in you now.
dancing.

being held.
laughing.

Form Follows Feeling

You must have chaos within you
to give birth to a dancing star.
—Nietzsche

When at first you hear
    keys tickle the ivory
    and the trombones trill
you want to respond
    yet ankles and toes lock in dumbfound woe
    on feet that once made it from crawling
to upright despite shaky tumbles
    recovering too from wobbles
    in a tavern's thick thunder
those brassy slipups trotted the next
    day into the field, lab, or law office.
    Later still, stepping out to theater and travel.

A journey of a thousand miles begins with a single step.

And so, you enter the dance studio and watch
    the speech of feet and you think
    let this be boundlessness
you will learn this, yes you will
    until the dance teacher says
    do not look at your feet.
So instead you begin counting
    one beat, two beat, repeat
    the construct of moving these damn feet
you can't help looking at—his, hers, yours—
    and the smiley teacher says again
    do not look at your feet.
Flustered, you forget his command along with every fluid cue
    flushing your mind to get out of the way and then, it happens:
Shazam! You feel the tip of a drumstick pulsing
    in the tender animal of yourself, folding into
    canyons of sound, riverbeds, a mirage of clouds and stars
and you swell into springy bones of your being. Being here. Now.

All My Summer Tans

all my summer tans
come back
in a Mexican minute

of sand, the heat of hope
skin curing like leather
in sizzling white light

fruit drying: my head
a bowl of fire with night music
guitar and trumpet fingerings

vast tomorrows with
torrid neverendings
of a heart falling in love

Salsa Lesson in Mexico

In a dank, ruined room
   air hot and still
      light bulbs waver
and the floor hammers down

A frayed pink towel
   in the instructor's
      curvaceous back pocket
catches each beat

Driven by drums songbirds
   ribbon-grass   skin-like glass
ratchet and hip clicks

Sweating and sliding
huffing for air
smolder and passion

O Baby, for
the seizure of the night

Floored

The honey . . . of earth both comes and goes . . .
—Wallace Stevens

Something is changing. The Sugar Maple and Rock Maple have taken
the axe, wielded by a logger who hauls them to the sawmill where
a log-splitter does what it does, stripping and ripping wrinkly bark
of birdseye tiger, flame, wavy, rippled and fiddleback. Creamy curls
of sawdust fall softly, dusty yellow perfumes the air. Carole King said
she felt the earth move under her feet. Love did that to her. The trees
get ready as a bandsaw makes cants and flitches destined to become planks.
And after that, tongue-and-groove boards, one with a slot, the other a ridge,
will be shaped in order to join together. I suppose that's love, too, velvety
smooth with a sexy charming grain, those ballroom floors a century old.
Turns, spins, pivots and other rotations need such floored boards hugging one
another, floating, giving in to pressure of dancers pounding the floor
in a Viennese Waltz, Jive, or Beer Barrel Polka. I could say this releases us to the
centuries, to trees grown for me and thee, but how can this be, an age-old forest
of melody and sound, here, now, enchanting us on the other side of sawdust and
honey light.

Angel of Joy

an angel of joy
rode the crest of her pelvis
and held the baby

riding side-saddle. his feet

nudged the mom jeans, his
hand the lace bosom

the angel whispered when
to wrap or stand or sway or
take a Mama-nap

I'm hanging on to you

like faith, the angel said.
I will be your rock
while you roll

down the road
with Papa and other
mortal creatures

Nine O'clock at Night

     The elders went to bed
why is beyond me and no doubt
beyond them, too, the reach across the
sheets, a release before sleep which
I'm told old people do less—the sleep,
I mean, just to be clear—for they awaken
several times during the night to sneeze
  or pee or count sheep, a metaphor
for all this night before them
and instead of putting on the Ritz, burning
up the dance floor, they've up and gone
to bed, pulled the covers up to the chin
and when the rooster crows to wake them
they're already up staring at a long day
when I hope they go shopping for
limber feet, racing hearts, elbows linked
to the stars, neckbones oiled and ready
to gleam in lacy racy see-in-the-dark
skin of the next night

Comprehension

Dance comprehends
through the senses.

The point of diving off a raft
is not immediately
to swim to the shore.

   It is to be in the lake
   luxuriate
   in the sensation of water.

Do not work
  the dance.

The dance will work you.

Let it.

Legs & One Other Gift

It's a rainy, foggy morning
claims the radio host—yet outside my window
neither rain nor fog, only
stone-cold grey, the sky ragged and tattered
as an old denim dress

So, I slip into my springy green skater dress,
fit at the hips and flared at the knees,
after Peter Bryant
on WPR's Morning Classics plays
"The Recollections of Ireland"

by Moscheles, a tonal postcard for piano
and orchestra, fantasia and sweet blarney

bringing me backward to ancestors

who live in my dancing legs, vibrant
and full of the dickens

like an apparition
given me in milk-paint light
when I visited the Emerald Isle: the surface of the sky
was endless with watery fog, foggy water, when powdery faces
appeared with eyes dancing in and out of focus, a slow kind of spell,
shapeshifting, popping an eyeball from one face, gliding it to another
nameless and ageless in longing (how long is a DNA strand,
might it splendor me as Aine the Faery Goddess?), a parade of dead heads
their flat faces stepping on and off the astral plane

no emotion whatsoever
a dull brilliance that was wildly enticing and it didn't make sense
to think about it so instead I received, hell, I welcomed the enchantment as

I watched them watch me, their heads tilted like flowers in soft wind, how they drank me in
studied my every move

animated and curious about what I was

doing with my life

while I thought this, of them: Stay with me. Stay.

The Leaves of November

this year, pale gold leaves
hung around

like dancers at the ball
toes tapping
fingers snapping
hips in hot spirits
long after
summer stopped playing
and autumn caught a cold

Sundance

The body says what words cannot.
—Martha Graham

Dance is more than ignition

It carries legends and tales
to fuel itself

covers the ground
in every country, the smoke
of every culture

clutching at oxygen
two little atoms enjoined to rise and fall in a breathy
        Viennese Waltz
        Polka and Pow Wow
        Polynesian Hula
        Russian two-step and Irish Step Dance
            a barn dance, square dance, record hop,
go-go dancers and Kabuki dancers, Kalamatianos in Greece
the Cayuga nation and ten thousand more in Africa, the Caribbean
since around the world

        The Sun Is A God.

And dance, therefore, the best expression of deity.
The sun exists forever   but   not we

rattling breath in a strawberry dance or blackberry dance
to feed us with

the very hot
hand of God
eager to touch, too much.

Ecstasy

A climax
is a little death.
A dance
is a little life.

— Frame —

When the Kissing

When the kissing comes
at dawn of day
mid-morning
past high noon
there is still time
all afternoon
to drink the sun
braid the wind
and
as evening comes
accept the gesture
of your hand
and hold it
hold all of you
what the rumba instructor
calls frame which
brings us back to kissing
a union of parts to
shape the craving

The Bod God

Dance, dance, dance,
little lady!
Leave tomorrow
behind.
—Noël Coward

the body is the temple of the soul

on loan
to us for a short time

My body is my joy
My hazard and
My responsibility
    Martha Graham said

so show up with your body
and I'll bring mine

dandelion or daffodil
pick me
for life just shortened as you read that

the trailer rusts, barnwood goes wormy
and the carcass of a deer lies in wait for the crows

but you!—you in your creation—own an engine
of knees and toes, joints to bend, cosmic chin,
starry arms to squeeze and
a broken heart, allergies, wheezes, stomach woes
take what you got before the getting is gone

pump it up, tone it down, move it all over town
wrap up the gift of your body
and give graciously
give with vision

out of this world
the flesh in flow, sanctified,
a benediction to receive
    humbly

Farmhouse Window at Night

A simple thing
to leave a bedroom window open
a crack at night
letting out
sour breath of sweat
whether rain or snow
a symphony of pines
cooing over storms
brewing in the house

And outside, a coyote in charge,
a cranky owl in the oak, the sound treetops
make when they touch the sky
humming over backache, fatigue—
his lungs scratchy with chaff, her hands chapped
starved for sleep while a deep
web holds the stars together
mist and dark birds
a faint far-off call
oh, vague white flower of a moon
on cloudy nights
a pearly one on clear nights
draping her collarbone, that doubly-curved beauty bone
long on dreaming
of country roads winding their way to the ballroom
where Saturday night thighs

once again waltz through whiffs of lilac and cedar
slide and glide to a higher plane
suspended in an order of magnitude
beyond measure

The Thing About My Father

was how he loved my mother
not with good works or good deeds
or even with good living—what
could a farmer do but promise
a freezer packed with a sow and a cow—
the house a constant struggle for my mother
to clean, a wringer washing machine, barn overalls,
clotheslines whipping in the wind with
white sheets she would later iron
for after they came back from the dance hall
where he had taken her in his arms and
she went easily, then, no argument about how
the waltz and foxtrot were warm-ups
with his flushed face, broad shoulders,
springy knees and fiery eyes
leading
while she followed
      until they got home
      when another dance began
      no linking of ribs
      no chickens come home to roost
      only squawking and hen-pecking

Sense of a Woman

My mother never
promised me a damn thing
not after she promised to love honor and obey
not after she failed to love
honor and obey the pistil in her own flower
a fact pointed out to her   by The Pope
noting a red-lined, black-stained fact
flung by her own mother too due to the infant
in a soft belly bulge when she married   when my grandmother wore
a rosary like a necklace which was not bequeathed
to me nor the silver fox stole she wore when I was a little girl
with me thinking a hunter had swung a carcass around her shoulders
though the message was clear: don't be a fox, keep your girdle tight,
do it in the dark if you must but only in arms
blessed by a man in black who never—so it was said—had sex,
speaking of which became a chore for my mother
her admission late in life when she claimed the queen bed
and slotted Daddy into the twin in the den
none of which thank you was lost on my scent
as I placed a box of Dutch Masters on Daddy's little bedside table,
reveling in how my own flesh charged when touched, when choices
dawned delirious as college jaunts, painted nails I later learned were called
fuck-me nails, traveling on trains, nude swimming,
Scotch on the beach, fire-red lips
a peasant skirt swirling around tight tan thighs
the Dutch hotel's neon sign glowing like a poppy
my wrist curved just so when pouring strong coffee in the Alps,
that nimbus of light in the valley and Kirlian colors reading not minds
but spines and hip clicks,
jet-black hair sweeping his forehead like a kiss
strapless topless braless—Less Was More—was blood-borne perhaps
since my mother was happiest when dancing, she said, those two impossibly
joined things: man/woman, gravity/lift, glad/sad, cold tears/hot ones,
soft womb in a bony pelvis, birth then death,
an animal running and an animal skinned,
larynx to lungs, speech into silence—my mother's troubling recurrent hoarseness.
Still, good luck when a bird shits on you
circles and triangles of prayer and rage, friendship and dread,
memories made up, the enlarged heart of hospice.

My grown daughter asks, what did your mother want, really?
She wanted to find herself, I say, form a life after graduation
raw and adventurous, dance jitterbug, join the Women's Army Corps,
nurse those wronged and mad
instead of being mad herself.

So I take it back when I say my mother never promised me a damn thing:
she promised me the heel of history, the blast
of time beneath our feet, bodies magically linked
unbuttoning desire and dance
with me in a heated trance
      for us both.

Some Times

Some times there is not a right time to dance
so if you know when and where that would be
tell the rest of us and we won't go there
doubting as we do there could be such a place.

Portrait of Rush

When your body touches mine a rhythm note sounds!
How can I move without it, my heartbeat at last found.
O! That you would ever caress and tease me
through leggy days and lazy moonlit melody.
Stay with me on the track of time where fancied
lovers savor one another like snazzy jazz candy.
Is there another world beyond our sacred present
with sweet gardenias in the station heralding our ascent?
O! Tender love god, gift us with endless eyes and sighs.

Carry us through cities of the sky, one stop after another,
Fedora hat and classy heels in lush novel summers.
Before we learn of either causes or losses in an era near,
let me wear my bones and you your skin of steadfast cheer.
Swell our brains with the scent of sex, throb, and rush.
O! Copper light and Cuban rum, vellum shoes and Chanel gush,
drape our trust in silk, chiffon, bracelets and bows, a chance
to flirt via ankles and toes, entwine thighs in blithe romance.
Whether Rio or Madrid, nudge our love to strut its stuff.

Dancing Tips for Women

1. You are always right on the dance floor.
2. Because the first step you take is with your right foot.
3. After that, learn to follow the leader.
4. Also (this is critical): learn to spot a
       leader about to whip, flip, or trip you.
5. He's out there.
6. So learn to move with the music, not with the manic.
7. Yet, remember, no one truly leads in dance—
       the motions are interdependent, synergistic, mutual,
       associated, and symbiotic.
8. But let him believe otherwise.
9. It's just easier. Trust me.

Dancing Tips for Men

1. Bathe before.
2. Dress in natural fibers to absorb sweat.
3. Get the frame right; the rest will follow.
4. Dancing is connection—
5. Connect with style, not with steering.
6. Body awareness (of yours, not hers) is key.
7. There is no need to think, count, or bounce.
8. No one watches you like your own ego.
9. Refrain from garlic the day of dance.

Fairy Wings

What is love, anyway?

Puddles of pain.
A deer in tall grass licking afterbirth
off a newborn.
A spasm of thunder before
driving ache.

It might be a stand of trees
defiant
and hard-nosed.

Might it be every seed in the sunflower
or a loon diving beneath
the surface of water like a submarine
plunging to the depths
hasty and rash.

Oh, please, let it
be easy:
daydreams
and feathery edges
of fairy wings
the kind
dancers sprout
to fly out of shadow
into the orbit
of trust

Full Body Chess

When I'm sixty-four, you'll be older too
sang the Beatles

and then we will
play chess on sixty-four squares

with prickly pawns, a crabby king,
that queen haranguing the rooks. Even
the bishop will blindside the knights
   just to checkmate the opponent.

The real opponent is time, however, so
      yoga up
         release the grief
            advance the divine
               and down the carrots.

Next, cue up The Beatles and dance, mate.
Dance and swing and dream as four mop-tops sing
      Send me a postcard
      Drop me a line
       Birthday greetings bottle of wine

Facial Recognition

the woman's
brown face
a coconut
seamed and scored
by sunburns

until she smiled
and then

her craggy lines
opened on coastlines
of former beaches

corners of her mouth
morphed into castanets
her eyebrows
waved and danced flamenco
ten thousand nights
of duende
love or lack thereof
pain joy passion anguish

fiery spirits
that would slither around
her ankles
and flame her belly
a hue and cry
at every revolution

How Can Red Be?

Human metabolism rises
when we come upon red
  apprehend and
  seize it in all its bloodlust, beauty, exultation

How can we not?
   In strength tests, a red light causes
a considerable increase in strength

and a red tablecloth, red plates
red dancing dress, red bow tie or cummerbund
bring out the season in every soul,
attracting luck and joy, the color of choice for a Chinese bride.

And yet, every bright side thing has a dark side, red
in a political sword will lacerate, cut a crying path to violence
and Russian roulette, a fact dismaying me since red is/was/will always be
my favorite color
to paint good humor and good will.

Consider then, the lusciousness of red, the vigor of its hue
in red jewelry or a red vest adorning any skin. How can this be?
It's the best-kept secret.
Red
  is the color
of the interior of the body.

Hey, red turns us inside out, red
raps at us, floods as we disremember the clots awaiting
every human being, urging us to take a chance now,
stop wasting time and take time and
   open yourself
   to one another.
Not to slander, but to tousle, gloss glamorous.
And to make an embrace
bold and powerful even with the pouty ones
    who crave a steady blaze of seductive dance
      and feel too blue to ask you.

Flicks and Turns

We were thugs, thieves
caressing in the bordello
    my ribs your guitar
    and your porteño frame a barroom rail
that bandoneon in push-pull
very velvety very sad

As we rode the tongue of night
hanging on one another
like a slide trombone
our arms chased shadows
our thighs in plush lush rush

O! Sweet liquor and smoke
ruffle our lips and churn our hips
in figure-eights
while piano and violin strum
    and we lunge, my leg slithering up your thigh
    your fingertips feathering my cheek

Let us play off one another in a balance of imbalance
reeling between seizure and purr, pulsing flare
flicks and turns in Tango
the tumescence of time when we drove one another mad

One helluva way to hallucinate
when we were thugs, thieves

May I Have This

Dancers are messengers of the gods.
—Martha Graham

May I have this dance, one asks, the other bows
and after that, flesh joins muscle and personality lends shape

his collarbone a pillow and hers a pearl,
arms and charm catch the drift

of brass and woodwinds, a peppy piccolo, pieces of piano
in well-timed measures between
throaty clarinets and a star-strung harp, back-up drummers
and a sultry singer

rousing up dancers

floating in the twinkle,
fall-away to ladies' fan, promenade, or pivot with back-spot turn.
Mambo and salsa will pick up the beat. Watch overhead lifts in swing
    torch the beams, this is pure physics, in passé, en pointe,
    any way you see it, oh, feel it!
                          as dancers
                              make
                              take
                    and create
              luscious scenes
        sifting stellar crystals—
          dust motes, really
            though dancers

think they're bolts from above
numinous messengers of the gods hand-carrying
marvel / flare of light / runnel of spine /
Hermes' lust and Aphrodite's dove love

in brief glory traveling through space and time
ancient and primal
intense points of intimacy and expression

living myths
    to believe in

when souls steal away to   *dolce far niente*
             (the sweetness of doing nothing)

O Solo Sad Farewell Dance

I heard
you were going
away
and I never
had a chance
to say goodbye

Maybe that's
the way
it's meant to be

for in my mind
you will never
go away

and I will
never
say goodbye

— Timing —

Tango Suite in D Major for Piano and Violin

I try to Tango
without you
teasing airspace in my arms
while the violin sobs
        and steam
rises from the piano

                But it is futile
                this burn in my heart

                Passion takes two

Where Would You Put the Fire

I wish I had danced more.
—Roland Sardeson, Mineral Point potter
(1946–2016)

Seize the fire from your kiln, Roland. It is not too late to sizzle.

All dance is love.
      All love is a dance.

Take me in your arms
    and say
        larynx
        lung
        toe
        tongue.

And I will do the same for your
          ankle
          arch
          pelvis
          pore.

We will connect in a two-hand hold,
read reason, moonlight, the origin of blood gush
in a soundscape surrounded by chaos—
      the catastrophes of life
          noisy fire
          fiery noise
of trumpets trombones
double bass and drums
while we speed across the ether
        climbing like Mercury, aglow with Venus
in the boogie-woogie jump blues:
combing the clouds
in throwaway moves and jig walks

for when lift plus thrust is greater
than load plus drag
anything can fly!

Because the Power of Dance
Lies in the Ability to Take Someone
to Another Place,

start in a room of strangers
with a stride, a tease: here is an earthy theory
of movement arriving from faraway solar flares,
fierce wind, fire in the plexus
        on a historic maple floor aligned with story

a galactic stage where players deliver lines
without words, touch becomes talk, and shape
creates meaning from those becoming weightless
as they dance past the body and
        reach the other side of the known

surging to trip the very memory of birth,
that first push spilling glory, uncontained, incredible
gain when he embraces her arms and she, his,
minds in the spine and rainbows
        rising like swooping birds

limbs linked when her torso wraps his
and his, hers, since neither lead nor follow in this
transmutation. They morph into one, a pull so perfect
        whirring the sun and purring the moon

before they bow in grace, a barely measurable bend
of wind to a butterfly far away who shall land
on a shoulder and mark the sky inside them
        the upness of blithe and alchemy

Delectable

The dance teacher likes breakfast at eleven:
rum and Coca-Cola, it being too early for linguine.
One evening at the bar, he tells me
he knows this means he has a problem
and dancing is not one of them, a slaphappy man

with a body-brain that can switch from
lead to follow, from follow to lead,
each done with smooth cool the way
breakfast runs into late lunch, the juice
of Coca-Cola splashed with aged dark rum
bringing in Caribbean rhythms and

an energy transfer as if the power
of dance needs to wander elsewhere
and fill an idleness between dance
lessons, the fun of bubbly harmonizing rum
for a floor craft wizard who teaches
hundreds the math of dance, how to

take one delectable condition and divide
it by a register of emotion to find
complex spontaneity and rap
through hours until shadows of night
when sugar snacks of rum and Coca-Cola
smack him, half-stepping and offbeat, home.

The Quarantine Started

Nothing happens until something moves.
—Albert Einstein

The quarantine started with a trembling, ringing note—
   thought bots chomped, chopping up dance cards and

      formal balls, no mirror ball to tell the future
      though some consulted crystals and chimes.

One man said a muscle test proved he'd be immune.
   A woman rubbed thyme oil over her body every day.
   Some dug deep into pseudoscience potholes.

Get your red-hot zinc here,
   stock up on coconut cream there;

determined to play this game of cognition
   to embody the motion of subatomic particles.

At which point, you wonder how thoughts entangle,
   how one attaches and influences the other.

You can't see a brain organize itself,
   or form actions, patterns or expectations

      like playing connect the dots,
      linking motor control and cognition—

but you can dream of the floor like a sea
   and spread your long wings toward it,
you can be Iris, messenger to the gods, traveling
   at the speed of wind from one side of the world to the other,
      down to the ocean's depths and to the underworld

or you can be Hermes, carrying secret messages
   with his winged sandals, purse, wide-brimmed hat, and caduceus
      the god of transitions moving between mortal and divine

riding the flight path into a time when you *will* hold hands
   with another to herald the end of storms after scientists
      court coronavirus and teach our cells new moves

When the Ballroom Went Dark

When the ballroom went dark
all angles and peaks
I darkened too

doom like a funeral dirge
grief and gloom

and then from within
I heard a familiar whirr

wind in the tunnel
between throat and heart

tympany and tempo
pounding inside—
a pandemic alive

but you and I, too.

Shuffling Through Sorrow of the Worst Kind

      Partners in class used to switch
like pictures at an exhibition, but this putting one face
in front of the other during a pandemic is not a competition
for the girl with the pearl smile or the boy with loose hips.

      This is a dance framed in fear—arms around
the vastness of space, the sound of one hand clapping,
an elbow like a kite attempting to ascend while weighted down,
wondering what current to ride next.

Jazz Poem You Didn't Write

Acting like our spines are in prayer position
        because
if you're down on your knees
        it's either break dancing
          or something broke

Bee Hive Jive

Inside a stack of white boxes
honeybees bop to a spanking-hot tune,
using gravity to indicate how to find food
by flying in relation to the position of the sun.

A relationship researcher discovered
a marriage had a better chance of surviving
if partners call one another by a pet name.

The hip-shaking waggle-dance of the bees
goes straight up, legs pumping a message
to other bees: fly *toward* the sun to find
flowers, nectar, drink yourself drunk.

My parents called one another Honey, then spent
fifty years stuck, arguing over who got whom pregnant
that fatal first shotgun time. Beer was involved.

A straight-down dance of the bees—imagine
dips and drops, jig walks and throwaways—
sends a message to humming hives:
fly *away* from the sun to find fragrant fields.

At the end of our vows, my second husband suddenly
swooped me up and carried me over the threshold.
A hornylovesick crowd cheered his sexual frankness.

Henceforth, when honeybees swarm to a new colony, take
their cue and start movin' and groovin' to ratamacues
and razzamatazz, let trumpet and sax fly *you* away
to a sweetie who will feed you, be your buzz.

Poised

Her ankles in satin ballroom shoes
will realize heaven tonight
when the music swells

and the question mark
of her spine becomes a metronome
keeping time with a partner.

Muscle memory from dance class
twitches like a tic and
she is ready for release,
smiling a winning smile
available / yours
though by now the waltz is half over
while she continues to sit.

Love is like that,
hungry and hopeful—
each partner needy and greedy
for flint, fire, a smoky pursuit
made complete by

a pair of shoes paired with another,
a match made in half-notes and whole
she thinks,
feeling the reverb in her chest
as dancers glide by
the light flickering

and
dreamy in degrees as she smiles
the practiced smile as she must
available / yours
until

the timing is right
to remove those hellish high heels
and leave
before the tuba's last moan.

Enough

is half of a Jewish idiom
as in enough already
and
for some items
yes we have had
enough already
of high-fructose corn syrup,
yellow teeth, beer breath,
dog farts, and alternative facts.
And yet,
what about an eon—have
we had enough of an eon
to plead
how we want
enough electricity.
How many transformers
and linemen will it take
to keep the lights on
and the band playing—and
how many light-years
will it take to illuminate
how we curve around one another
after the dance
lying side by side
still in motion.

Angle of Love

Love, there are no questions left for you

I have seen you in rage
unshaven face
in a crowd

How you once enticed me
your mouth a glory
a buzz saw

How I savored you
until you chewed
me up and spit me
across the floor, down the stairs.

In other words, love, you are made
of sweet licorice, black moods and
alluring danger I often

felt when the cage of your ribs
rattled and we hugged
one another
opening one another in flavor
or maybe opened *to* flavor

because love, when you held your tongue
and opened your guise
while the band warmed up,
mercy (that old beggar) tugged at us

in a rotational pattern resembling
a back spot turn to cross-body lead with inside spin
how it seized you and then me
vacillating for three minutes
as the bite of language, the kick of history
let go—how, for three minutes
we forgot what we were fighting about

busy as we were
in the old soft shoe, the limelight of what
we once had and for those three minutes, wanted more

Last Night I Danced the Tango

And my partner had air
in his shoes, smooth.

And my waltz partner said
you're a lot of fun to dance with.

And my fox trot partner said
dancing with you is like
driving a sports car.

And all of them held
me in grace
and I was fuel, flame
the energy in my arms
empty with you as I
gathered the music like
a minesweeper

> the battle in my heart
> crossing the floor, dodging
> memories of our
> kicks-with-attitude, ronde,
> our seemingly endless
> wrap-turns

before we dipped, tripped

the flint of old hurts flared
      and
when you served
me the papers, your hand touched
mine briefly before
our rollout-to-attack
where we took our positions

and the burn began
      our fiery last Tango close.

Slow Dancing

When the earth started its pull
on my father,
he went, a willow would,
shoulders cracking,
knees cranky—where's the chair—
unless a big band came to town
laid reality at his feet
each ankle and toe-tapping beat
asked for a dance
and got its way, he
nothing but a wisp of wheat
able to get up the Irish
in my mother, take her
across the floor, smooth
her feathers except
the morning he found
her on the floor, eyes
glassy from a stroke,
did he ask for one more
dance and she gave
him a stare,
a look of something longed for,
or lost.

Delirium

When my father's
gasping begins
I cradle his hand

already cooling
blood having left
his extremities and

drained from his cheeks
the blood-thirsty heart
pulling the last love

I want from him
as he heaves, wheezes.

And I place my ear
on his chest
hear the heart ache

while the transistor radio
tucked aside his pillow
plays Big Band, melodic notes
thrum on his lips and form
a flirty half-smile.

Surely he is coming around the
corner of the dance floor
while Engelbert Humperdinck
sings *The Last Waltz*.

I turn up the volume.
(Hearing is last to go.)

After he passes, that waltz tune
is stuck in my head,
on repeat.

Intention

Only come to me
if you have suffered

if humanity has hit you
so hard it rots your soul

Come to me
to share your shock
your rupture, crack, or craze

Come dance with me
connect with me

Come to me in fine turns
and quicksilver lines and
       we will give ourselves
       to the dance floor

We will leave it out there
after our bodies speak

with emotional phrasing—
no one can teach this

You learn it in a state
of shock, shutdown

the memory of joy
in the state of grief

Becomes an invitation
to dance and we accept

for when there are
no words—you dance

Inductive Reasoning

I think therefore I am.
I am therefore I love.
I love therefore I dance.

I dance.

Therefore,
I am.

One More Reason to Dance in Case You Needed One

You
owe
it
to
the

world

to

become

a

better

person

— Becoming —

The Poet

I thought of becoming a poet
when I was growing up
but the job description was vague,
pay too paltry to pay the rent
and I wanted

> strange accents, mad dancing,
> falafel and baklava,
> *nasi goreng*

but in meat-and-potatoes Wisconsin
making a living from words meant
that one day
I might have to eat them
and
after seeing my brother sputter
on a mouthful of soap

(the preferred method back then
to cleanse accurate expression)

I wondered how my words would taste
and
I decided not to become a poet
although
there are times
I still think
I'm doomed
to be one.

The Atom

      For every positive
there is a negative
physicists claim

      protons and electrons
but I the writer
am a neutron

      picking up particle bits
from the man and woman
in divorce court

      the teen and his gun
the foreigner
in a foreign country.

      When you split
the atom, you will find
me in the center

      full of them all,
more, quite frankly, than
the center can hold.

      And so, I explode.

Of Blue Fire

You write like a woman who has not read much.

I studied his hard lines on my midnight work
and worried. I did not know New Formalism,
French critical theory, or deconstructionism.
I knew a path the cows took home,
how they found their way
without the herding collie.

I knew too, gas stations and beer stations,
full of men for teasing and receiving,
read lips, touch hips. And I knew
Mama's drift—*Find something, young lady,*
to fall back on.

So I fell into nursing where curdled screams
reached those delivered
and bleeding and nodding like members
of a secret club.

It wasn't a book club.

On days off I tried to read like a writer, but
Baltimore harbor bars,
daylong drunks
yellowing my rowhouse walls, thieves
splitting oak doors to nab my stereo and TV,
leaving behind fiction and poetry

I longed to sit and read—read until the cows came home.
But Williams Obstetrics and Neonatal Resuscitation
(not Whitman or Nabokov) staved off liability
that grew from love
and lust
that made those bursting women
(some still girls) pant
until they couldn't. Then, they screamed
      blue fire,

pushing themselves inside out while I kept watch
for late decelerations, shoulder dystocia,

other marks
to mar a newborn's lifetime.
And now an effete teacher had made me
the outsider dropping splice commas
between pain spikes,
quoting Apgar scores, exclaiming
done blood, placental release

raptured nipples
ready for the keeper or adopted,
palsied or an infertility win, none
of them minimal, surreal, or post-modern,
only a down-to-earth assurance
that back home, black-and-white Holsteins
navigated from the pasture,
udders pinked full, eyes fixated
        not on the stars
        of their ancestors but on the ground,
        that gravid, welcoming ground.

Cornfield

I love Iowa City in summer. I love *en plein air* and sandals and verbs lost in backpacks. I love lazy bicycles and serious beer. Detail rules. Apply it on trees; aim it at the golden dome and river of young and old. Stamp poetry in cement on Iowa Avenue—*keep a diary and someday it will keep you.* Walk on words and feel feet in charge instead of a cerebrum at-large. Iowa City is Greenwich Village in a cornfield. Till the soil, oil the plow. And grow, goddamnit, grow.

Stage Presence

for Tim O'Brien, Captain, Comma Police

Usually, but not always,
comma wants its way between breaths of air,
usually *little* breaths;
let *medium* breaths suck in semicolons.
Usually, but not always, comma gives the limelight
to a period, usually, but not always,
when the actor takes a
big breath, when enough has been said.

Until,
an afterthought nude of all punctuation enters stage left
and manages to be heard in spite of the actor's speechlessness
and deplorable lack of breath control.

My Doctor Age 96 Tells Me

Back then, they were called tramps.
My mother reheated food and
put it on the back steps.

That's a good house.
Stop there.
Can we mow the lawn?

They weren't white-collar
guys, they were street people.
And they were hungry.

September Inning

Under bright baseball lights
    boys turned golden
in a setting sun

Girls on the team
    waxed fair
haystacks of ponytailed hair

and in a moment of ageless grace:

        The earth revolved
        The game went on
        The grandstand stood

when every eye locked
    on a high pop-fly

when we were America
and everyone had a chance to play
for it was about pure play
when that September inning
arrived and

it was enough
before it wasn't.

Fingerstick

So a man disappeared,
       last seen in a bar,
       the exact time unsure.
       Times flies when you're—never mind,
       a man disappeared. This happens
       more often than you know; flesh and bones
       discovered weeks or months later
       to examine DNA from lips and thighs,
       anything that once was alive. As for the man
       who disappeared? It happens everywhere,
       but this the first for our small town,
       and at Bugsy's the next night
       yakkity-yak about how no one
       really knew him, he didn't fit in
       not even with jukebox din.

       Some surprise he was diabetic,
       those brain cells famished and
       the fingerstick too late
       for a body craving sweetness,
       a little cheer

April Air

That morning in Memphis
azaleas in pine beds
        rose
under hot high skies and the Oldsmobile
stacked with Wisconsin white girls
        hellbent
on white beaches, white light, Daytona
drive all night, slurpy sleep in no AC,
the blonde behind the wheel
careening toward daybreak and April air
        bursting
with daffodil shoots, amorous and
oh so sweet until city streets
        erupted
with more black fists than
the girls had even seen, a mob
out of nowhere
        body-slamming
the windshield, pounding quickly locked
doors while bottle shards flew.

The spring-break girls spun
the radio dial for information but only static
        reeled
through stations, no explanation, the UPI wire
still asleep in days before 24/7 news,
the suck and rattle of the Olds
        slowed
to a crawl, ticking, Firestones hissing,
even pansies and dogwood
        disturbed
by nonstop slap-whacking on roof and hood

hundreds of hands jack-hammering
those lily-white girls
        trapped
in the fact
that the Doctor with a dream
        was dead.

Afterward in Two Rivers
a tribute to 9/11

Afterward used to mean pushing
back a chair at the table,
for conversation, a cigar or maybe

it meant the spent look on your face
when you were still inside me,
freed into sweet belly breathing.

Or recall the best afterward at
the bottom of Suicide Hill, after
my sled went faster and farther

than anyone else and my squeal
held in heavens above. But now,
dare it mean apple-red cheeks

after we labor to fill bushels with
Macintosh, Golden Delicious,
and pride before F-16s rumble

overhead to protect the nuclear
power plant not that many
miles from where, afterward,

wild turkeys and their babies
step through tall grasses,
gracious, cautious.

Heaven

At sixteen, the good kiss
relied on pitch-black darkness
during the seventeen-mile ride to our dairy farm
after we won the basketball game
and my point-guard boy danced with me

to *Oh, Pretty Woman* in a dimmed gym—
what kinesthesia that dimness held and
again in his father's Ford Fairlane downshifting
through country stop signs, the landscape
dressed in see-through black underwear,

a chocolate sky, our talk tactile and tantalizing
while we review a full-court press, mockery over
the history teacher in the bleachers desperate
to get laid and finally we're at my half-mile
driveway, headlights pick each stone as we inch

our way to the farmyard, arriving breathless
and expectant; the Ford nestles between the pump
house and granary, startled pigeons fly from the silo,
two barn cats slither from one hideout to another
as his arm reaches for me and we wriggle in,

windows steaming, a period of study begun
when suddenly the yard backfills with yellow light,
a naked 100-watt bulb under a silver saucer high
on the cow barn, the switch thrown by my father
in his drawers shivering on cold kitchen linoleum.

Within twenty years, that 100-watt bulb
would yield to fierce halogens, and jet-black
undulations on a rural drive would sallow
into urban sky with our earth gone electric
and heaven losing its mind.

On Being A Farm Kid

From six to thirteen, Mama drives you to school
with siblings banging lunch buckets, calling shotgun.
From fourteen to eighteen, you're riding a yellow bus
of future farmers, homemakers, Marlboro men.

Who can recall their faces, the one who was gay,
the aromatic ones straight from milking
or slopping hogs? But you leave them
for mountain climbing, theater, jazz.

Perspective doesn't know where you live yet,
only advertisers, the wallet starting to bulge
with memberships and plastic, promises of better
living through chemistry and mortgages—

you can't *Just Say No.* At the travel agency,
you peruse how wild turkeys poke in the plowed
land, a skunk labors up and over each furrow,
and shadows lengthen over white-tailed does.

Rural Route One: a travel destination you think
unique and beautiful and fabulous. In the glossy,
light beckons a road with no end. Dutch elms
look fake, too tall, yet the canopy waves and

in the distance, your father walks toward you,
knuckles swollen, hands full of arrowheads.
Look what I found, he says, winded
from plowing, eyes wise, all of him avowed

to leave the earth the way he found it

My Mother's Kitchen

Beneath the butcher-wrap paper
lay formica of gray with black flecks,
and after my mother and her side-kick

Anita finished wrapping T-bones, round
steaks, sirloins, blade roasts and pot roasts,
they lugged in a 20-gallon pail of ground

chuck and slapped and laughed the meat
into patties, placing thin squares of paper
between each patty for ease of separation

when the burgers would go from freezer
to frying pan, before they taped an outer wrap
and dated it in black—my father's

job would be to rotate packages in the freezer,
designate which heifer in the barn
could not be bred or milked or sold

but by next year would end up dead
in my mother's kitchen while she and
Anita yakked and yakked, grateful

for the homegrown kill, the time to restock
the freezer for ten mouths, slaving
till sweat circled their arms, the little caves

between their bellies where they found
space to gossip about the sweltering summer,
the upcoming dance with a polka band,

a shotgun wedding, *I Love Lucy*,
and the growing pains of children
none of whom had yet gone vegetarian.

Rummage

Rummage. Was it a noun or a verb?
To my mother, an early bird arrival
at every display, it was both—

      an adjective too
      Rummage Sale signs
      luring her like a casino

where she gambled
on dragonfly bird feeders,
Legos, summer clothes

      for the kids for next year
      plastic pumpkins, Disney décor
      crocheted pillows,

dishes shaped
like pineapples
for quintessential yellow Jell-O

      sweaters, pants and
      tops she scoured
      and scrubbed

but her second-hand fever
fever stopped at the shoes:
beat-up tennies, ratty sandals

      boots with manmade uppers,
      heels worn down like an argument,
      my mother not wishing

to walk a mile in someone else's shoes.
She had corns and calluses
enough of her own.

Angel of Simplicity

Simplicity was the pattern-maker
        onionskin we would
        cut/cut/cut
        for bodice skirt and waistband
the sleeve of the future, my mother said

enrolling me and my sisters in the
Cleveland Merry Masters 4-H Club where
we learned to sew
flat-fell seams, gather skirts, line plackets

design a time to do something
do you know what it was why
did it take so long to find it was
I asking the wrong question
or was it
        simply
        (a derivative of sim-pli-city)

how I feared to ask that   or   more
since my mother would harrumph
past the ironing board on her way to
the washing machine
and call me *argumentative* while I begged

her to stop working
sit down talk with
me or at least buy
me a dictionary

        so I could look up
        argumentative

The Dying Farmer

Act I

Put me where I am useful
just beneath the topsoil
half-inch down of warmth
and wet loam in my hands
pitch me a shovel or rake
let me get up when the sun
splits land from sky and blazes

There's work to be done

Act II

Tell me to rest when darkness falls
though I keep one ear to the barn
where the calving goes
when the sow spits out piglets
like drops of water and then rolls over
on one or two short
happy lives

If I'm not there to save them
put me in marketing or
production or design
and teach me a fresh use for duct tape
the brave new ground

Act III

I want a part
in a pioneering play
and I'm fine to be
the living tree on stage
with no lines to speak

The Mechanic's Wife

She is exhaust in the room
as he grinds one bolt
threads another and
fills the grease-gun
with amber thick stick-to-it-iveness.
With each grunt he creates
friction. In the shop's shaky light,
he squints, stops only for a
soda and a cigarette, fires
an air-gun while her ears shriek.
He fills the house with stains that
preach since she has yet to come to
him willingly.
Soon the sun will beat
through the pane, pour crystals
on the calendar girls he keeps nearby.
She will bleach his fingers
with kisses and talk dirty,
swear she likes it
gritty and extreme.

The Waiting

Inside a box
nailed to a shadowy peak
   of a cabin
on the shoreline of Peninsula State Park
furry-winged bats hang
in upside-down dreams, no light,
while bicyclists zip by, lovers swat lies,
and little kids get lost and found in lush green lore.

            At dusk,
precisely as the last sunbeam slips
off the lake, hundreds of bats
whiz from the box to lace the sky, swooping
stars of an airshow. Some campers
duck when bats head toward them, some joke
how they too picked up speed in night's bright
freedom, flew on booze, pot, or sexual tease,
willed cars to fly or lovers to leave.

But, oh the flicker between revere and fear
for us edgy over nights yet to be seen:
high-pulse parties and fields of teens
when we find a child's bed empty
and swoop into the black hole
of waiting—flying on blind faith

Michigan Avenue Trestle Bridge

How lonesome rode that whistle train
Each note afloat on the river near
The conductor leading a grand campaign

The tracks ahead were bold terrain
For anyone with eyes to hear
How lonesome rode that whistle train

While a trestle of stone and steel reigned
The truss piers of 1906 held high and clear
The conductor leading a grand campaign

Hauling the makings of America's brain
The dream of transport, much to cheer
How lonesome rode that whistle train

The speed of commerce would be sustained
If markets and profits bulged every year
The conductor leading a grand campaign

The Chicago-Northwestern he entertained
His reward let's hope a Kingsbury beer
How lonesome rode that whistle train
The conductor leading a grand campaign

One Hundred-Year-Old Tree, Now Gone

Of course it wasn't gone
when he painted it in 1981. . . he had a vivid imagination . . .

      Still, could he have known
      the tree would come down to put up a building

he was hypersensitive to beauty and nature
it strained him, his emotional gauge
went up and down, he lay awake at night
with the deep colors of the lake
and the sand and the fleshy full tree

front and center
in his sense of time

was it the water or the shoreline or
the peninsula in the distance where his second child
had been born or was it the tree itself

bent by
westerly winds
that called help me, pick me, paint me

      I am old and leaning
      into a superb sky

      I am hope and desire
      when grief gathers in the heart
      like water in a swamp

      I am the color in nature
      leaves grey-green, some yellow with black
      the sand a smattering of burnt sienna, ochre, and umber

      In high wind, I suffer without complaint.
      I am pain without repugnance.

There is neither good nor evil in the world
but only being and doing.

      You are being a tree, doing your job.

And he is being a painter,
not painting to sell but to seek

to make *mooi* against terrific odds
        mooi being Dutch for beautiful
and it was   all of it   until the day of *doei*
                which is bye-bye in Dutch
Bye-bye, Beautiful Old Tree! Thank you!
And *Doie!*

An Old Woman from Arles

A woman is not old
as long as she loves and is loved.
—Vincent van Gogh, *Dear Theo*

It is in the eyes
where love resides

Vincent could feel a look
time travel like in a book

recounting what love could do
when it colored a mood

it paraded the brow
it insisted, Here, Now

it left echoes in bones
a holy and hellish loan

to an old woman still whole
and while Aristotle wrote, *No excellent soul*

is exempt from a mixture of madness,
your brush, Vincent, lifted a soul's sadness

your hand and eye so sublime
I'd love you anytime

Sunflowers

I think that life is pretty long…
—Vincent van Gogh, June 1873

Sunflowers stand
by the hand of the sun,
staunch lovers
who grow rapid, go deep

in Dutch literature where
the sunflower is a symbol of loyalty and devotion
       and Vincent lonely for a future Rachel

bled for beauty, gazing at
fields of turning heads with pinpoint seeds
staring at vases of petal velvet
begging three shades of yellow, thick brush strokes
      of impasto
        luscious as a buttery beach, canary island, and bees

the symphony of yellow inside him
enduring downpour, drought

      and even rejection—
      a pest with no cure
      that would in time gnaw
      at sunblind stunned butterfly love

How risky to have a dream
of unison and trust

Sunflowers don't last that long

Vincent van Gogh died in 1890. He was 37.

Life Drawing Class

She offers
   herself up, nude
Nervous, curious
   and broke.
A pretense
   of grace
As the pose is set
   denial
Of a ripple of chill
   across her clavicles
Spasm in the great toe
   and up the
Knotty rope astride
   the spine
A siren while
   artists gaze
In the name of art
   amazed by the strange
And wild thing where
   bogs and shapes
And coastlines form
   pools of light
On her full exposure
   a shimmer
Only she knows
   as shiver
When she holds
   stock-still
Recalling love
   left in the marrow
Shadowy quick lines
   for shoulders
Holding up hope
   pancake breasts
That fed others
   and a belly
Sagging with mudslide
   grooves—
The lived-in-look
   of where
Her babies
   grew.

Telomeres

like time ticking
during deer hunting season
telomeres on a chromosome shorten
with each cell division
until dead and gone
and
soft light
when the sun is fading
requires the experience of witness
a connection with nature

parts of me are older
    than the sun
I am made of
    supernatural parts
I could be the woolly steel stag
running in rut   head-on into my auto

Oh luminosity
All artists are obsessed by light
A deer obsessed
An obsessed deer
    leaps   crashes   explodes my hood

Headlights of truckers and travelers
whiz by   no one sees
the stag's supernatural parts disperse
        the floating belly of night
        when nature hits the ditch
while I am left behind, the one
    still running
the split eye obsessed
    to connect
with bony rays of moon
strumming telomere strings
after the deer flew   flaring   dividing
the singed air
the night's mosaic
        eating his shoulders and shank
            and my ticking heart

— Being —

Applause, Applause

in a sense
we
are all

clapping

our way
out
of the audience

Eyeball

what I
see

cannot compare

with what
I
feel

Handful

       they said
it was all in the cards
but it wasn't
it was in   hands that held
the cards
cards in hands under stars
       and
the stars illuminated
one simple fact:

you spend your life
with a handful of people

Plunging

A flock of pigeons can bring down a 747
but not today while window-seated I soar
through padded, push-up clouds

that remind me—they amputated *both* her breasts.
I had heard about it in the shoe department
when I hurtled through, putting things

in order for my trip, a high-heeled, open-toed
number to match a low-cut, sunny dress.
I'll call, send a card, I promised to her sister

who gave details including, no visitors now,
she's out of her mind, fiercely sedated.
I gave scared condolences and took off

to erotic reds, adjustable straps, lipsticks,
Panama rose lingerie for sleeping or sipping
and thinking about breasts and babies,

about lovers and fashion photographers,
about a greeting card for breasts in search
of a sunny dress, about a card to comfort breasts,

those twin engines, the ultimate in matching
numbers for killer nudity, riveting lines you can't
take your eyes off, whether there, or gone.

We Don't Talk About It

I come from a long line
            of
we-don't-talk-about-its
            since
talking involves feeling
            and
feeling is a thing
            you
cannot change
            so
why talk about it

For the Eighth-Grade Girl Writing Love Lyrics

There is a line you will cross
in the ninth grade or the tenth
quick slip of judgment, addling after
The Boyboy you wrote about in eighth grade. That
boy or a different bothered boy will stir you if you
let him tell you what you want to believe. Study his
rhythms and those of the agent, coach, or music
marketer telling you how to dress, who you ought
to be between the measures before your body
becomes someone else's body
not the bright-eyed trusting blessed and
testy one you need for your first album
and all the ones thereafter

Who the Virgins Are Not

Not the postulates dusting the crucifix in April
light, eddying toward Easter, not the fusty librarians,
not ballroom dancers of vicarious pleasure, not
the babe on first base, not the pom-pom chick
with VD who wants to be born-again, not *The
Virgin* by Klimt. My friend Aggie says her name
means virgin but knows the original etymology
of pure portrayed a woman complete unto herself,
genuine and natural, intelligent, a wild spirit
with no need of man-made rules or fantasies to be real.
The dire link of pure with sex came in the Middle
Ages from men in swishing black petticoats. Men, akin
to the Gothic word *manna*, perhaps from the
root word man, to think. Perhaps, not.

Who the Doctors Are Not

Not the one telling you it's a melanoma,
not the one unclogging your cholesterol, not the
one exclaiming it's a girl, not the tearful
one reporting the first-grader has leukemia, not even
those self-proclaimed rug doctors, or crazy
doctor DJs, or the lively ones cracking your back.
When my husband looked at me from the
span bridge that day, the Mississippi rampant beneath us,
I threaded my fingers into my daughter's hand
on one side, my son's on the other, before their Papa
tossed me the car keys and went so far afield, he
landed in another country. It was my friend, who had been
through the same sameness, who across tea at her table,
beer at mine, opened her throat like a bird, and healed me.

Purring

The key in the lock was a channel opening
to song when the career girl entered
and a cat named Freeway jumped off the sofa,
it was like a pass from Bart Starr, lasting
thirty-three seconds or less and time wasn't
the subject the surety
of connection was the point
and when the fluff of fur died,
the career girl opened the door remembering
when love itself greeted her.

Freedom Fighters

      They are coming.
And they are young.

They are yellow and red,
white and pale.
They are black.

      Blue.
And they are coming.

They are green as olives,
adding their numbers,
subtracting their numbers.

      They are gung ho.
And they are coming.

They are brown as nuts.
They are multiplying,
subdividing.

      They are young.
And they are coming
home, one piece at a time.

The Renter

She came back with bloody scabs
and a lost limb, thinned. She
unraveled but had to go on.

And so, she started out by renting a tiny place
across from the Dairy Queen, a two-room shack
slathered with brown paint
for an earthy sense of home. Occasionally, she sat
on a metal lawn chair, smoking, wearing
a black Tee, blue jeans, and steel-toed
I-can-kick-your-ass boots.

That first winter she put an American flag in the snow
and it blew away.

One day she loaded small logs into a rusty
wheelbarrow. She rolled the wheelbarrow
to the corner of the small lot. She stuck a sign
amidst the logs. The sign read, *Campfire Wood $10.*
The wheelbarrow kept its load all winter.

In spring she rolled the wheelbarrow behind the
lean-to and planted a black flat wooden silhouette in its place,
a soldier down on one knee, with a gun. She added purple
and yellow peonies at the kneeling knee.

By summer she got a Harley and parked it on the gravel drive,
there being no garage. And then
one day a man wearing I-can-kick-your-ass boots arrived.
He sported a swollen belly and wore a belt buckle
the size of a pork barrel. The setting sun
caught an earring in his left ear, twittering. The two
of them trolled around the Harley, advancing and retreating,

cocky and perplexed. They both wore sleeveless black Tees
and now one could see the skin of their arms had been punctured.
Designs had been inserted with indelible colors. They told
a rousing story of dogma and certainty.

In fall, the renter planted a flag the color of stone
next to the black silhouette down on its knees. The flag contained
a round black circle and white cross-bones.
The lawn, a patchwork
of quack grass and bald spots, yawned.   Someone donated a black Lab to the renter
but mostly the dog bounded around the property like it wanted out.

Thirst

the saloon was the watering hole
where folks went
come hell or high water
when they were in
hot water
deep water treading water
with a jokester
who was a long drink of water
and the girl in skinny jeans
could be counted on
to turn on the waterworks
for they were all ordinary folk
filling one another with story
flowing with metaphor
each in their own way
trying to quench
        their thirst

Touch

it is warm and willing
it is cold and chilling

it is flesh
and
it
wants
so much

X-Factor

Each of us are born with X number of words,
X number of heartbeats to be used
like a MasterCard or Visa credit line.
Surely you're familiar with the guy
finishing the golf game and *whoosh*
he's gone, or the race car driver
taking the big one behind the wheel,
the dancer on the floor, the pilot
in boiling clouds seared by the sun.

Then, too, term limits, X-files,
and how many X-squared heartbeats
squeeze into rounded-up minutes
on phone plans, X's crossed by marketing slams.

But no one imagines X number of
WORDS
those pre-numbered words and yes
that includes translations, so don't get snippy
about mortality, it wasn't my idea,
all these interruptions with dial-up or DSL,
bad weather radio reception or rude sisters
who don't let you finish . . . as I was saying,

if we only get X number of words, the worst
would be to run out in mid-sentence
or during an emergency, but then that's
the beat of it, the asyncopatic beat of it,
asystole, the ultimate flat line
each of us some day will cross.

The Ambulance Driver

Let's say
it was his propensity
for speed
that led him to apply

      to roar
      in the left lane
      whistles and sirens

spewing
fear for the one
on the stretcher

feel the fear and race
at a hundred miles an hour
red and blue lasers
gas on someone else's dime

while the soul on the stretcher

bobbles along
with
a random thought

      the ambulance
      could become
      a hearse

for both of them

At the Know-Nothing Party

A good time was had by all.
They played games . . .

> Blind Man's Bluff and
> Cops and Robbers.
> Their favorite was

Tag, You're It.

The merrymaking died down
when there was no one left
to bluff, rob, or tag.

Hate

Hate is such a
heavy word.
You have to lift
a lot of weights
to bench press hate
to throw its discus bulk
half the length
of a lifetime
or
to come upon it
with surprise
and say something
like I love you
and wait and see
if hate will still throw
its weight around.

Because We Are At War, Here Is Advice On What To Do Tonight

call someone you love

and listen
to the sound of lips
when they kiss
each word, each urge—
hear the baby's cry,
sirens, tales of daffodils
and ducks, jeers, a joke
or two though no joke
how you hope to lope
into tomorrow

when, you promise,
you will call again

Fraught in the E.R.

They each drink 36 ounces
of water before starting
a 12-hour shift,
then guzzle
another 24 ounces midshift:
this team of masked rangers
armed with know-how and
on the lookout for
an outlaw named Corona
with barely time to take
care of themselves.

Grilled Cheese

I have to love a sandwich so
greasy it could condition my hair,
oil a hinge, seal a poolside tan

I have to love a sandwich
that knows its limitation
yet spreads it like a rumor

a sandwich that bows to the blow
of grace, smacking its lips
for sweet Jesus & cheeze Louise

a sandwich with the sass & sleaze
of a fat cat denying a heart attack
a sandwich so beautiful

it bathes in butter before lying down
between white slices of heaven
a sandwich that is surely enraptured

that can do the do-wop like a
brave little sermon, a sandwich
with a soul of sizzle splat, got 'dat

Fondue Party

Of course my request comes
with reserve and good sense
that you fondue me

fondue being the feminine passive
past participle
of the French word *fondre*

      to melt
though I must tell you

that while I am not   a passive lover
I do savor the idea
of melting
in a communal pot   with an oh-oh-oh
little flame underneath
a flame Americans call Sterno

while the French sing out *réchaud*
a spirit lamp
the god of combustion
a transformation of food
designed to enliven your slumber
your sails, your wee buttercup inside
with gastronomic gusto:
    such hunger you have for a
winsome and winning life

and how are you shaping that life
do you blaze behind the third eye
waste your wildness on argumentation
    wonder why you never took up belly dancing

though one could argue
there are different forms of that
I have seen it in the garden of eating
which brings us to this communal time
where my best manners   beg you
to keep me warm—almost hot—but not

so hot that I burn, yes yes, I am a picky lover
not given to upset or heartburn

begging your fire

for you give light
I give desire

Sister

My sister doesn't do sad.
She tried it on a few times,
        different styles, different sizes—
        nothing quite fit. Either too loud
            or too dark, too tight or too baggy, she'd say.

But I think it was the silence of sadness
        she couldn't size up.

See, she's a musician and she hears
        B major (the happiest of notes) in her rose garden
        and she weeded out E flat minor (the saddest)
from between the beans
        because she lives
            in the key of wonder.

When I was little, I watched her
practice piano on the windowsill before
    we got the upright
and now her fingers glide on the bass clarinet and she loves

parades and dogs and actors on stage.
She bakes toffee bars, chimes in at
book club, and will call you on the phone
checking in with perfect timing and then

        when it gets too quiet

she will sit at her kitchen table
and hand-write a letter

to a prisoner

so when it is opened, her cursive flows like a cello
deep and smooth making a little cell swell
words rise from the page
    like high notes of a flute

measure by measure
my sister's drum roll of love

        piercing the
            silence there.

Squirrel

Brown squirrel
  on white snow
    a silhouette

erect and alert
  scanning
    the lay of the land

preparing to meet
  the nuts
    in the neighborhood

Paper Towels

Paper towels. She asked him to pick up
paper towels when he went to Menards.
He froze, stock-still and glanced out the
picture window at the catalpa.
The rain was already upon it.

Paper towels, he said and she braced
for a speech about wood pulp, reforestation,
use of rags, the inconvenient truth of waste.

But instead of a three-point argument, he said, *Paper towels*.
Yes, she replied. *Paper towels*.
He chewed his bottom lip; his molars
seemed to grind. *Paper towels*, he said.

This went on for minutes, three syllables bantered back
and forth until he asked, *What are paper towels?*

     It was then she turned, viewed his face,
     eyes cloudy, eyebrows flat, deflated.
     He could have been on a sailboat, rounding
     the Horn of Africa, a storm gathering,
     and not known it.

She described paper towels, the dispenser made
of Vermont maple that he hung beneath the cabinet, how
he used them to clean windows, wipe the oil dipstick, sop up
grease from the Weber.

     But he was still in Africa, shoulders braced
     against pelting words, the pencil in his
     shirt pocket stuck, a rusted compass he could
     not use to direct paper towels—*My God*,
     she suddenly thought, *can he spell anymore*—
     to his shopping list.

She hesitated, about to write . . . something . . .
on his list until she imagined him run aground in
aisle five, in irons, the approaching cold front
tangling his sails. And so

without another utterance, she gently waved him
to go and he went, his truck bobbing down the long
gravel drive as she watched and threw him a wish.

For Cryin' Outloud

the ICU now a Covid ward
and from behind masks
nurses swim against the tide
gasping for air
begging supplies as they
check flow rates
safeguard tidal volumes
measure oxygen percent

day in and day out, after the noon
and darkest night   there dawns a
healing touch through gloves
voices coated with empathy
but it is their tears—their tears—
that bathe the breathless

Riff

It began in the body, always,
chocolate spooned around white,

an afternoon smelling of rose and tangerine
and above us, a bookshelf swollen with stories

of pilgrims and slaves, legends
in disarray while we talk velvet,

touch plush. I feel your arms around me
the historical weight shaking, *please*,

want me. Then a fall-away of incandescent
fluorescence when you write:

blue is a hue you cannot choose.
Blue is a riff, I feel, that handpicked you.

Now memory plays scratchy tunes in late
afternoon, deep-cut roses bending to light

while I consider how love grows on the inside,
pulsating and pushing the blood, red luscious,

though in that Syracuse, it ignited pelvis
and spine, shoulders and waistline: earlobes

and retinas gushing everything right
until walled by your mind, tangled in fear,

cursed by the times.

Sparkling Points of Light

In the halls of my house
I see your face: every feature
a fine art painting
                wanting wall space.

Take, for instance, your wide smile,
cheekbones high with ideals,
the lid of your right eye
                lowered like Van Gogh's

as you squint toward a world
where the work stalls, the gallery rejects,
the back rent backs up, and you burst into a fit of rage
                that fairly shakes the walls

while I stare at sparkling points
of light in your eyes
hear how an artist must be selfish,
                guard every second of his working time

a scheme crash-lands in your lap, on your face,
you iron your moustache as your right lid droops
lower and you want to be happy with
                horsey-back rides, chess, and swimming

while treading water with credit cards and car repairs,
happiest when you do not think of unhappiness,
Sometimes I can't stand myself, you laugh
                with a wit quick and genial

and then the doctor gives you lithium
you feel so normal you cannot paint
the silence hard in your heart
                when you go to walk the dog

recovering to taste a sweet orange sun, feel the rain's blue cool,
ponder the sliver of a moon, the luster of a woman's skin
hue, tone, tint, and shape so intense, you weep, knowing
                you must wet your brush and paint
                what only you can see

This, I Believe, Is What You Are Telling Me

Get a view.
Preferably a long one.
Short can work too.
Roar.
Growl if need be.
Judge no one.
Heat up.
Cool down.
Light a candle.
Listen to the body.
Favor circles over straight lines.
Wash your hands.
Check your pulse and then thank it.
Paddle through gossip.
Make big splashes.
Skip often.
Anoint your feet.
Mind the stars.
Mend torn thoughts.
Avoid compartments.
Be wrong.
Come closer.
Seek solitude.
Crack your back.
Expect the unknown.
Love with ease.
Laugh a lot.
Do not lean.
Be beautiful.
Be fierce.
Be anything but mad.

How To Be Happy

Do not compare yourself to those
        around you.
Eat a perfect soft-boiled egg.
Wear a baseball cap backwards.

Learn a skill. Snuggle.
Keep a window open year-round.
Lose with grace.
Be kind—others will be kinder to you.
Giggle.

Become aware of breath—yours first,
        then, others.
People who hold their breath will
        try to steal yours.

Share.

— Dreaming —

Make Up A Language
In Order That I May Know—You

begin the no
        (now)
the no
        I cannot see how
it's an end of
        the road
        situation
the end of all
how (long) is end?
when I commit to memory
        you laughing
        a long in-
        fectious
slam
        dance laugh
        a (downright) siz-
-zling trance
and you   never saying
        good
bye
awful guttural sighs
after I can
        (not)
find my feel
        (ings)
this is not happen-
        (ing)
is not fade
        (ing)
cannot feel the stop
is not topped the
        (stop)
        still
            where and when
                (how, why) hue and outcry
over your steely strong
        arm
the tennis serve
        so sweet
to a spot

now
dim
    (ming)
so, no not now
not ever
can I sew syllables for the letting
    that lets you go
to the next dimen-
    sion
love unmatch(ed)

your space
    place   there
my place   here
    punctuated
tiny holes (leak-ing)

[love ain't nuthin' but a bleeding dove
and the eagle   still   a loner]

while the scalpel blade
of a path-
    ologist
slicing through skin thin(ned)
cuts into guts—lung, kidney, thyroid—and squeezes

that heart at last stilled, spies the fiery brain
    c o o l e d
truly, damn damn damnit ice-cold
    and (   ) and, what?—
what will there be   (elsewhere)
but throbbing, pounding, rumble thunder

hear(ing)
    you lift
    (ing) (making)
surplus laughter
rolling long laughs that
last
and last and
last until
    (smash)ed

Master Critical Thinking
With A Baloney Detection Kit

I grew up with baloney.
   I did not like baloney.
        In summer, it sweated in wax paper sandwiches.
        In winter, flecks of fat hardened in my lunch box.

Baloney, after all, is an afterthought,
   remains of organs pulverized to minute particles
   pasty as Elmer's Wood Filler
   with a scent of leathery wet work boots.

Ah, you say, you're full of baloney,
narrow-minded as a Democrat,
arrogant as a Republican.   Wait.   I have not gotten to taste.

Alone, baloney tastes like ambiguity,
   the perilous fallacies of logic and rhetoric,
   a simple fare of food that, alas, lacks common sense.

Thus, mustard stands at the ready to coat it
and, on a kind day,
   bring together conviction with compassion, strive to see
   another's point of view, combine
   sweet pickles, onion, mayo, and yes, more mustard.

So, there's one theory of baloney. Are there more?
   Multiple working theories have a better chance
   of becoming the right answer than swallowing the first one.

Another theory touts the nutritional value of animal fat,
   salt, nutmeg, coriander,
   allspice, celery seed, and black pepper.
Another, artisanal expressions in German baloney,
   mortadella,
   rag baloney, and ring bologna.
Another, the human need for nostalgia, that hillbilly
heaven in the mind at Rural Route One.

And yes, let's revisit, you're full of baloney, an idiom that speaks
   to underlying fears—the fears hiding inside
   beliefs that seem acrid and bitter, unreasonable.

How can I find those fears, become the best baloney detector?
Who will guide me? Guru? Historian? Philosopher?
Shall I arm myself?   Or shall I bring out my razor:

Occam's razor, a rule-of-thumb to urge me,
            when faced with several theories
                        that explain data equally well,
                                    choose the simpler.

Either that, or switch to calf brains, stewed tripe, or fried liver sausage.
Though honestly, I can't stomach any of them.

I feel worried, confused.

It is then I hear a knock. Open up, it says. And I do.
It is my heart, bursting with love, urging me to connect.

And I do.

That does not mean I am in thrall to you, baloney.
Nor, that I like you—
though it sure helps me forgive you.

The Lawn and Those Adirondack Chairs

a chair for you
a chair for me

and we shall
lounge

in poetry

And So, The High School Quarterback

       The praise must be lavish
and over-arching, quite obvious,
even the unschooled grasp that,
but the nuance is the slight turn of the wrist
slant of an eye for this guy, the king of the mountain,
untouchable, lovable,
the one who calls the shots and then
stands back, cheeks squeezed and unscathed
as he watches the pile-up
this life lesson with a pigskin single-handedly
tossed into future deceptions, ego of a pigskin
which, actually, is made of cowhide

Orange

for Frank O'Hara

One day I am thinking of
school: The Art Students League,
I write a line about the halls. I have
never seen the halls of the League. So
I write about the windows, the mortar,
the staircases. I cover the stairs with
cigarettes. Days go by. More cigarettes.
I am a real smoker. Suddenly it is
1970 and I have been there seven years.
I am painting. I am winning scholarships.
My teacher Edward Laning gets
exhibitions. I get more paint. I make a
painting so big it comes in four wooden
parts. One day it ends up in an exhibition.
But the gallery put the pieces together
wrong. I called it Puzzled. Though the
way it is put together, it could be
an orange, too.

Street Clown

what luck (good or not
depending on belief)
there's a clown

up ahead
while streetwalkers
rush hither and yon

and a clown bends the
rules of normal reality:
a magical possibility

you may choose
happiness or fear
out of colors and clothes

paint your face
with an emotion
that suits you

Firefly

I
The firefly shows its iridescence.
The night is dark.
This June is wet and way too cool.

II
Often the fawns are drunk with newness.
In their world it's just one hobble after another.
It's like looking at puppets with dancing spots.

III
You and I have spent so much time escaping.
We've known for a long time what we were doing.
It's okay if we admit to pleasure.

IV
I am so in love with dark chocolate
that I don't bother looking for imposters.
The smallest sliver satisfies me for hours.

V
I long to see the rich river of cocoa and
the flavor-maker urging the high notes to come.
I saw her palate awash in daily wonder.

VI
You and I escaped the life of the drones.
We love to remember the way our fathers
managed against all odds to find the sweet spot.

VII
I will get out of your way while you rub your wings.
I will watch your beam color the night.
We will write the dawn just when it breaks.

Commitment

Oh, I'm yours
you know that
but my way of keeping
is not yours, stuck to ribs
breath rushing
from throat to lobe

> My way of keeping
> flutters behind my third eye
> a butterfly
> near, then far
> until . . . tired,
> I light on your finger.
> You offer shade.
> I bring ardor.

Loving The Line

I loved the long line
of cars with headlights on
in the middle of the day

nearly high noon
line crawling behind
a police escort

and me going the opposite direction
slowing to a crawl with them
car after car filled with wet faces

who stopped their world
whose world stopped

out of respect, shock, anger,
relief landscaping the terrain
on a random day to make me

make eye contact with each driver
before I scan the back seat
looking for remnants, a hat, scarf

had someone embalmed the dead
on Facebook, the ultimate haunt or
a voice on video, a cell phone

greeting: Hi, this is Francine
leave a message
and I'll call you back

The Parting

what it takes
to leave blows in
with unease

a dull eye, cheeks
so gaunt and giving

lungs
awhoosh
and wooing

one can
almost
hear
the mourning dove's
soft lament

though it be dusk
when
your arms
reach out
like destiny

like a promise
to stay

the way an echo
will stay

how it is
heard
long

after gone

The Institute

The day after
I visit my daughter in prison
I think about where she lives now, how I'll never see
her top bunk, a bony mattress missing her Dutch duvet at

> Taycheedah Correctional Institute
> ready at the edge of ridges and rocks

Taycheedah
> from a Native American word that means camping place
> a flat Wisconsin site chosen in 1921 for the
Wisconsin Home for Women—she had an eye for hanging paintings
in her condo, could do it without a measure or level—but here
the frame is the Niagara Escarpment
> standing up
> > in relief
> a prominent line of bluffs

with broken slabs
of limestone
toppled together
rimming   the basin of a tropical sea   awash there
> > 400 million years ago.

> How small I feel standing there.

Wind
skims the cliff, lofting, singing
with tribes on nearby Lake Winnebago long ago.

> Walking toward the chain link fence
sounds rebound against walls in my heart:

> > Tell me, I ask, what is that curly barbed wire called?
> > Mom. Didn't you see *The Shawshank Redemption*?
> > No, maybe, I can't remember, I . . .
> > Razor wire. It's called razor wire! Anybody knows that.

Leaving, I approach the heavy metal gate, look toward the building
where I know a guard watches behind his shadowy reinforced window.
  I wait.
Soon, a clanging bang opens the gate
  and I walk through, wondering

can she, can I
rise up, drum out the cynics, resist erosion,
gather chunks of loss
  like love notes I once put in her lunch box

find a place in the legend
of modern motherhood

  and let groundwater seep
through our stone faces
bring cooling relief
  beauty in
  brokenness, still
  life.

The Bird

A little bird is singing on my shoulder
Every day I ask it: is this the day?
Is this the day I die?
Every day it goes on singing.
And so shall I, until I die.

Amsterdam

the golden light quivers
a finger stuck in the dike
holds back the mystery of love

Daytona Beach At Dusk

Walking alone
on the world's most famous
beach devoid of people and cars in January
years after you and I, here,
young and lost, walked past
Coppertone bodies bellies and biceps
muscle cars bubbling with mufflers
cascading waves   we heard as
only the young can
not knowing then   our dreams
were destined to collide
your bottle, my pen forever trying
to write the sun
squint to see unborn babies
on the rim who would
arrive a decade later
to me   without you
and then in time immemorial, a grandson
squeezes my finger. I am completely gone.
There's an irresistible force of heartsong daylong
a blaze of noon until out of nowhere, the news—
he is gone. Impossibly dead.
A toddler forever tangled in my soul.
I gulp air. My pulse thumps. Time goes granular.
But then he returns, pure presence, when I am near
water: fountains, rivers, lakes, the end of the ocean,
forms on the move, shifting, shaping.   Holy water.
The wind blows cool today.
Raw wind, raging wind, bone lonesome.
I tighten my wool scarf and tremble,
doused in an oceanic roar of grief
knowing you, my beach walker of long ago, are dead too
and I am left here with
ancient waves brushing the sky
baby-blanket-blue, smoky lemon, a smudge of lipstick pink
loyal constellations on the edge of lavender,
the uncertain purple curtain as Poe said
heralding messengers of the gods.
    And, I listen, hearing a tempo in the pendulum of time
for I am alive, breathing between octaves of loss, echoes
of melody and refrain, windsong nightlong
a neverending vibration of
longing—another name for love—
pounding the shore

Helen's Hairdo

Peace, my heart, let the time for the parting be sweet.
Let it not be a death but completeness.
—Tagore

Usually, it's Tuesday when Helen comes for this peace
in my beauty chair, girl-talk, tales of her life and my
marriage, our kids, and what can rip a heart

and sometimes, she reads my face when I let
her for she's everywoman, the bake sale lady, the
talker with an ear, a fixed gaze when time

stands still as when a stabbing cramp comes for
me just as she arrives with pale blue curls for the
set and style slot, except I'm in the bathroom, a bloody parting
inside me will not stop, will be
witnessed by Helen, who says I will drive you, come my sweet

and off we go to the hospital, a memory I let
lance me when her daughter calls, this time it
will be me both talking and listening, it will not
be Helen, flat out, lips sealed, eyes no longer to be
set on me in the mirror as I take my comb and fix a
strand, wrestle a cowlick, chat about cruises, recipes, death

how fast that cancer grew and grabbed at her but
at me too, alone as I spray her do into resolute completeness.

Back Story

It never is what you think it is.
At least it wasn't what you thought it was.
Or perhaps you were not thinking—I'll
        give you that—when feeling
        (make that feelings) take over.

        Overdrive
        an overdraft of passion
        for which there *is* consequence
            a fee or penalty

which is how the paintings on the wall
came to be after he disappeared

his timing self-serving and capricious
his only vision to spend his days painting
after he disappeared, leaving behind a pre-teen daughter and son
        who fell into a well of wishing
        drowning in disbelief, bereft
        of father-hugs and Monopoly moves

though never a loss of love, the love did not leave
when he did

remember it never is what you
think it is
        instead it *is* what it *was.*

The past becomes the present and tomorrow
twists memories of today and those other days
when joy bumps against grief, and hope swats at fear

because that's what happens
when a spirit beating madly
cries to the voice-over in the head

until heart and mind in concert
sometimes off-key, other times in glee
        make music
        of storms and longing
of the whisper paint makes when it touches the canvas   and stays.

Liminal

My daughter in prison plays the piano.

She plays from memory, eyes closed, her heart
a violin stringing along
as piano notes fall like raindrops
wrinkly soft while cedar trees and tulips
bend to her allure
there are movements
          musical interludes
her long fingers barely touch
one key before alighting on the next
rolling up and down, a lift
at first playful and soft, then loud
in a key of meaning while low sun warms the floor
and lingers like a kiss
a yearning, a longing
something called love.

Enliven it now, that memory, pick up the pace.
          See her at the Young Chang
as I round the corner and drive in the driveway
a 12-year-old practicing on the upright
so I do not park my heart at empty but at a
home flowing with Sonatina in G Major by Beethoven
a girl making music after her father ran away.

Except. She is only pretending
I will learn, much later, how her velvety blue bench cushion
became a launch pad to an alternate universe (somewhere between
fear and possibility) plucking at
ragged sheet music to smack the gut
in grief, threadbare shame stuffed
into a little cell with her life
little now, safe and contained and cruel, and family
claiming they can't fix anything, fade into silence.

Musicians say it is the notes not played that make the song.

Meanwhile, my daughter splices quarter-notes into eighths,
off-key, a symphony of stones, cacophony
as by now I imagine—wouldn't you?—she pounds
each key with fury
a bluebird fighting a crow for the last speck.

Stag

The twelve-point buck never
learned to count steps, cannot tune the digital
camera set on a stand by the weekend bow hunter
to monitor shanks and bellies, rollicking measures
of squeal and blare. Have you ever heard
the snort of a stag in rut, seen him
wag his rack and paw the forest floor,
stomping his hubris, headstrong
after a doe's dancing scent, her beautiful
big brown eyes a love-call sharper than
an arrow straight to the heart

Up There

a sliver
of a
moon

and me

glimpsing
the
other half

of you

We All Live On The Water

Everything you do is good.
Everything you choose and everything
That chooses you finds its place in
The bedrock, in the chiseled furrows
Of the earth between which water runs,
Gossip flows, waves of insight crash and splash
Like the sperm of your grandfather searching for perfect roundness
Which was not the moon
Was not the sun
Was not the globe itself but
Was a woman, her undulating lines running like a river
     slow
     lazy
     rampant
     raging
See how smooth her skin, her slicked-back hair
When she cuts through the surface tension.
See the boys seeing her emerge from a lake: dripping, delirious, delicious
Before she dives deep and deeper in search of age-old secrets—
That bag of amniotic water she carries before
She is a woman making breast milk and cake batter,
She is building snow castles, fishing
On a frozen lake. She is a dousing rod, a woman
With a tsunami of tears over ungodly news,
A hydrocephalic, a tire iron to the head,
The roaring faucets of need and greed.
And she is a woman sandbagging the levees,
Her garden washed downstream,
Or elsewhere, she is drowning in drought.
Nonetheless, she rises early or late,
Splashes in the bath, fills a teakettle, goes head first in the pool.
The force that propels her is ancient, perhaps Divine,
She has come from the garden
Into the house to wash her hands, to start dinner,
Dropping potatoes or rice in a pot of water, a cycle repeating itself
While millions of molecules move from earth to sky
And back again,
A centrifugal force of evaporation and condensation

That leaves your mind
Spinning, your body on its feet, singing
> Because everything is good, everything you choose and
> Everything that chooses you
Is water, the body sixty-two percent water
Floating in primordial space, breathing liquid air,
A Buddhist believing life is fluid and water wettest
When we inhale pain and exhale love
Enlightenment coming while we swish and splish and listen
> To the way it ends, the way it begins
> Delicious, dripping, delirious

Acknowledgments

At age fifty, I left a career in nursing to study writing, good fortune leading me to Dianne Benedict, Bruce Bond, Frank Conroy, Pam Painter, Gordon Mennenga, Sharon Oard Warner, Marshall Cooke, Christine de Smet, Mark Jude Poirier, Robert Hass, Laurel Yourke, Kelly Dwyer, Carolyn Forche, Katie Ford, Laurie Kutchens, Melissa Pritchard, Caroline Leavitt, and Jonis Agee: each one helped develop my multi-genre voice. For this, I am enormously grateful.

Heartfelt thanks for those who taught me the art of dance (Bruce Marshall, Susan Alby, and Rod Schultz) and for my best dance partner ever, Robert Gahl. Indebtedness, too, to the Wisconsin Fellowship of Poets, the Mead Poetry Circle, and the countless writers who journeyed with me, including Blair Deets, Karl Elder, and Sylvia Cavanaugh.

How lucky I was to be found by Cornerstone Press at my alma mater. Special thanks to director and publisher Ross Tangedal, managing editor Grace Dahl, editorial director Kala Buttke, production director Amanda Liebham, and production assistant Abbi Rohde.

Gratefully acknowledged are the editors and curators of the following publications, where some of these poems first appeared:

The 2017 Mill Prize for Poetry: "Fondue Party"
The 2014 Mill Prize for Poetry: "The Mechanic's Wife"
The Alembic: "The Ambulance Driver"
Amarillo Bay: "The Mechanic's Wife"
American Journal of Nursing: "Fingerstick"

Art as Poetry/Poetry as Art: "Portrait of Rush"; "When the Kissing"

Chautauqua: "For the Eighth-Grade Girl Writing Love Lyrics"

Carquinez Poetry Review: "Who the Virgins Are Not"

Confluence: "Rummage"

Cottonwood: "Telomeres"

Fox Cry Review: "Of Blue Fire"

Green Hills Literary Lantern: "Orange"

iris: a journal about women: "Who the Virgins Are Not"

Making It Speak: Poets & Artists in Cahoots!: "The Lawn and Those Adirondack Chairs"

Margie: "Freedom Fighters"

Owen Wister Review: "Of Blue Fire"

Peninsula Pulse: The Hal Prize: "Helen's Hairdo"; "Daytona Beach at Dusk"

Poetry in Color, Rahr Art Museum: "Michigan Avenue Trestle Bridge"; "One Hundred-Year-Old Tree, Now Gone"; "Street Clown"; "Sparkling Points of Light"

Porcupine Literary Arts Magazine: "Afterward in Two Rivers"

Portage Magazine: "Slow Dancing"

Rosebud: "The Institute"

Sheltering With Poems: "For Cryin' Outloud"

Slipstream: "Who the Doctors are Not"

Southern Poetry Review: "Plunging"

Spillway: "The Atom"

Spirit Lake Review: "At the Tea Dance"; "Tango Suite in D Major for Piano and Violin"; "Because We Are At War, Here Is Advice On What To Do Tonight"; "The Waiting"

Stoneboat: "Paper Towels"

The Summerset Review: "Grilled Cheese"

Van Gogh Dreams: An Anthology: "An Old Woman From Arles"

The Velocity of Love: "This, I Believe, Is What You Are Telling Me"

Wisconsin Fellowship of Poets: "Firefly"

Wisconsin People & Ideas: "On Being A Farm Kid"; "My Mother's Kitchen"; "Angel of Simplicity"; "Sister"; "The Dying Farmer"; "Heaven"

Wisconsin Poets' Calendar: "Thirst," "How To Be Happy"

Woodland Dunes: "We All Live On The Water"

The Yellow Toothbrush: "Liminal"

KATHRYN GAHL is a writer and poet. Her works appear in three anthologies, four ekphrastic art shows, and over fifty journals, with awards from *Glimmer Train, Margie, Chautauqua, Rosebud, The Mill, Talking Writing, The Hal Prize for Fiction and Poetry, New Millennium Writings*, and *Wisconsin People & Ideas*.

A Pushcart nominee, she served as Writer-in-Residence at Lakeland University. In 2019, The Council of Wisconsin Writers presented her with the Lorine Niedecker Poetry Award, and in 2021, her poetic memoir *The Velocity of Love* (2020) received an Outstanding Achievement Award from the Wisconsin Library Association.

An avid ballroom dancer, she believes in the power of red lipstick, deep sleep, and compassion.